LET'S VISIT BAHRAIN

Let's visit
BAHRAIN

S. & P. JOHASSA

953
HAS

ACKNOWLEDGEMENTS

The author and publishers are grateful to the following individuals and organizations for permission to reproduce the illustrations in this book:

Camerapix Hutchison Photo Library Ltd; W. Hassall; Spectrum Colour Library; Travel Photo International.

CIP data
Hassall, S. and P. J.
  Let's visit Bahrain
  1.   Bahrain – Social life and customs – Juvenile literature
  I.   Title
  953'.   65053   DS247.B24

ISBN 0 222 01093 2

Burke Publishing Company Limited
Pegasus House, 116-120 Golden Lane, London EC1Y 0TL, England.
Burke Publishing (Canada) Limited
Registered Office: 20 Queen Street West, Suite 3000, Box 30, Toronto, Canada M5H 1V5.
Burke Publishing Company Inc.
Registered Office: 333 State Street, PO Box 1740, Bridgeport, Connecticut 06601, U.S.A.
Filmset in Baskerville by Graphiti (Hull) Ltd., Hull, England.
Colour reproduction by Swift Graphics (UK) Ltd., Southampton, England.
Printed in Singapore by Tien Wah Press (Pte.) Ltd.

86 - 33

Contents

Bahrain, Pearl of the Gulf

Before oil was discovered there, Bahrain's wealth depended on a shellfish found in the waters around its shores. This shellfish was the oyster. It was not valued as a source of food but as a source of pearls—the valuable irridescent stones which are found in some oysters. Bahrain used to have a large fleet of pearling *dhows*—the traditional Arab ships, which went to sea in search of pearls. However, this was a long, arduous task and they were not always successful, for only a small proportion of oysters contain pearls.

How did the pearling ships of old manage to stay at sea for months at a time in the hot, salty waters surrounding Bahrain? A clue to the answer to this question lies in the name "Bahrain". In Arabic, Bahrain means "two seas". In times gone by, the pearling *dhows* used to lower large pipes made of leather onto the sea-bed. They would then send down divers to fix the ends of the pipes over bubbling freshwater springs at the bottom of the sea. The strength of these submerged springs would force fresh water from under the sea-bed, through the leather pipes and up onto the decks of the *dhow* to sustain the crew for yet another hot, gruelling day. Hence two seas—one of salt water above, and one of fresh water below.

It is the very presence of this pure, clear water which is said to account for the quality of the pearls to be found around Bahrain's shores which at one time accounted for the wealth and prestige of this island state. Although the harvesting of pearls is of little importance nowadays, Bahrain well deserves its title "Pearl of the Gulf" for, like the pearl, its size reflects neither the attractiveness nor the true value of this little country.

The Arabian Gulf countries of Kuwait, Saudi Arabia, Bahrain, Qatar, the United Arab Emirates and Oman all have a shoreline on the Arabian Gulf which separates the Arabian mainland from Iran and the continent of Asia. These countries, commonly known as the Gulf States, lie in one of the driest and hottest areas of the world but have all developed extremely rapidly as a result of the discovery of oil.

Bahrain is held, by many visitors and Bahrainis alike, to be one of the most pleasant of the Gulf States in which to reside. The freshwater springs in the northern parts of the island make it green and fertile in comparison with its more barren neighbours. This, in turn, perhaps accounts for the cheerful optimism of its people—the Bahrainis. Although urban development and the growth of high-rise buildings has lessened the significance of the age-old description "the land of a million palm trees", it is still quite possible to imagine that Bahrain—

8

A date-palm in Bahrain, "the land of a million palm trees"

blessed with the water of life in such an inhospitable region—just might have been the "Garden of Eden".

Bahrain has played its part in the modern world. Oil, which is the raw material for petroleum and many other twentieth-century products and which is also responsible for the tremendous wealth of the Arab states, was first discovered in this region beneath the sands of Bahrain. It is these same oil-bearing rock formations which are responsible for the high water-table. This means that water is found near the surface of the ground, and that many springs rise in Bahrain despite the high temperatures and obvious lack of rain. Rain which falls on mountains—as far away as the Zagros Mountains in Western Iran and the Hijaz Mountains on the other side of Saudi Arabia—is carried under the desert sands and saline waters of

9

An oil-well in Bahrain, the first Arab state to discover oil

the Gulf and up through cracks in the limestone. It rises as the bubbling freshwater springs of Bahrain—on land and at sea.

Although it is often thought of as a solitary island, in fact the State of Bahrain consists of an archipelago, or group, of thirty-three islands which lie in the shallow Gulf waters between Saudi Arabia and Qatar, just north of the Tropic of Cancer. As recently as 7,000 to 8,000 years ago—a short time in geological terms—these islands were probably still connected to the mainland of Saudi Arabia. Changes in sea level and a great deal of erosion have transformed what was once a great

10

limestone dome of rock into the present low-lying land surrounded by sea. The Jebel Dukhan—"Mountain of Smoke"—so-named because the heat and humidity of summer appear to engulf it in haze, is the highest land in Bahrain reaching a height of 122.4 metres (445 feet) above sea level. Although little more than a hill, the Jebel Dukhan is the most distinctive geological feature since it rises steeply from a depression which lies almost at the centre of the main island and is encircled by cliffs which dip away to the sea. It is also the site where oil was first discovered in Bahrain, and is the last reminder of a great fold of rock (which geologists term an "anticline") that existed in the not-too-distant past.

From the summit of what is commonly known as "the Jebel", the sea can be seen to both east and west. On a clear night, it is possible to see the gas flares of Dhukan in Qatar and, to the west, those of Dharan in Saudi Arabia—more than forty kilometres (twenty-five miles) away.

Most people in Bahrain live and work in the northern half of the main island (after which the state is named), and the nearby islands of Muharraq, which used to be the capital and where the airport now stands, and Sitra which has an industrial complex including the refinery. These islands are interconnected by a network of causeways carrying fast, modern highways which make it difficult to believe that once there were no alternatives to ferry-boats or wading at low tide. Now, almost everywhere can be reached by car in just over half an hour—traffic jams permitting.

11

The causeway which connects Muharraq island to the main island of Bahrain

In the north-east corner of the island of Bahrain stands the capital, Manama. It is growing at an incredible rate and pushing out into the sea as buildings are constructed on reclaimed land. This is the commercial centre upon which most of Bahrain's wealth now depends. Here are found the high-rise office blocks, the international hotels and the banks which mark Bahrain out as a modern influential state. This island is approximately seventeen kilometres (over ten miles) wide and forty-five kilometres (twenty-eight miles) long. There is a narrow cultivated strip five kilometres (three miles) wide along the north coast between Manama and Budaiya which produces local

12

vegetables, a variety of fruits and the traditional dates.

The population is concentrated in the north, round Muharraq, Manama, Budaiya and Isa Town, and extends down the west coast to Zallaq and Hamad Town. Originally, this was because only the northern areas had freshwater springs. However, much of the water now consumed is desalinated sea water or more brackish underground water which has had the salt removed. This has meant that the new planned towns of Isa Town and Hamad Town could be constructed in quite dry areas, involving less disruption for traditional agriculture and the village way of life.

In the central depression, just north of the Jebel where oil was discovered, is a town of wooden houses which was conveniently built as a camp for the oil-workers. South of this

Water for sale, from the 7-Up desalination plant

town, called Awali, the island remains an underdeveloped desert area with a few rough roads over the hard limestone rocks and occasional sand-dunes which lead down to the most southerly point of Bahrain. Off this spit of sand, called Ras al Barr, lie the Hawar Islands—a group of sixteen small islands which are largely uninhabited save for colonies of birds and animal life.

Another island, Umm an Nassan, has been connected to the island of Bahrain by one of the most exciting projects in the Middle East. This is the Bahrain—Saudi Arabian Causeway which links Bahrain to the trans-Arabian highway system and demonstrates the importance of Bahrain to those living in the region. Bahrain has always been an important commercial centre on the trading routes through the Gulf. With the introduction of air travel and the need to refuel, Bahrain has become a stepping-stone between Europe and the Far East.

Hard limestone rock in the desert area in the south of Bahrain

Climate

Bahrain, like its neighbouring Arab states, has a harsh climate. However, it is influenced by the surrounding waters of the Arabian Gulf. This means that temperatures are not quite as high as on the Arabian mainland; but humidity, which is a measure of the amount of moisture in the air, is generally higher. The summer lasts from May to October and it can be very hot and humid. The most unpleasant months are July to September when temperatures in Bahrain can reach 46 degrees Celsius (114 degrees Fahrenheit) compared with the Saudi mainland where temperatures of 50 degrees Celsius (121 degrees Fahrenheit) and above are quite common. Although temperatures are somewhat lower, the high humidity in Bahrain can be extremely exhausting (up to 100 per cent relative humidity) making an afternoon rest a necessity for most people. It is so humid that, for instance, glasses or sun-glasses steam up completely when the wearer leaves an air-conditioned car.

Air-conditioning, of course, has radically changed life in

15

Bahrain. Now, almost all shops and offices are air-conditioned and most houses either have central air-conditioning or separate units, the size of a television set, built into the wall of every room. Sometimes it can make the atmosphere so cold, in contrast to the heat outside, that people actually wear jackets indoors in the summer!

The winter months from November to March are extremely pleasant and temperatures average around 17 degrees Celsius (62 degrees Fahrenheit). It can also be surprisingly wet; although most months of the year are without rainfall, for a few days there may be an unexpected but real downpour with thunderstorms. At such times, floods are common on the roads since there is no system of gutters and road drains such as there is in ''wetter'' climates!

Strong winds, known as *shamals,* usually blow for several days. In winter, these winds sometimes reach gale force. In summer, a *shamal* is a welcome relief to the extremes of temperature and humidity.

Plants and Animals

Although Bahrain is a small island, it has two quite distinct habitats for wildlife: the northern fertile region, a strip of land which runs along the north and north-west coast, and the southern desert region. Even within these two habitats there are different areas which attract different kinds of wildlife. Some plants and animals are found only in or around the plantations, gardens and freshwater ponds of the north; some only in the desert conditions of the south. Others, like the sparrow, are found in both areas.

The water, vegetation and shade of the plantations attract many insects, beetles and geckos. Geckos often live in houses and are very useful because they eat all kinds of insects. There are some snakes, very few of which are poisonous. The grey mongoose, introduced from India, is skilled in killing snakes and has kept down the snake population. It also kills rats and shrews but probably does not tackle the spiky Ethiopian hedgehog. There are also two species of bats. A large colony of them inhabit the ruins of the Portuguese Fort. Others have found a more modern home and cling to the high-rise buildings of Manama.

There are many birds living amongst the greenery of the north. Perhaps the most spectacular are the green parakeets which often visit the gardens in search of sunflower seeds. Hoopoes, bee-eaters and bulbuls are other attractive birds which live in the plantations. Barn owls, which fly out to hunt at dusk, are often persecuted in the Middle East as they are thought to be messengers of death. Round the ponds of the north live frogs, terrapins, herons, egrets, bitterns and a variety of ducks.

The desert region of the south (which may, at first glance, seem quite barren) has a large variety of desert plants, although some of them may need searching out. One plant that is easy to find is the solitary "Tree of Life"—a thorn tree which stands in the desert, far from any other vegetation or visible fresh water. In the winter, after the rains of January, February and March, many plants seem to spring up "over night" in both the open desert and the *wadis.* *(Wadis* are dry river-beds which sometimes become flooded in the rains.) One of the most beautiful and unusual plants to be found is the pink desert hyacinth.

A traditional symbol of Arabia, the gazelle, can sometimes be seen in the south. It used to be hunted with Saluki dogs— the Arabian hunting dogs—but now gazelles are protected because they have become so rare. The *dhub,* a very large lizard, makes its home in the desert as do the desert hare and hedgehog. There are dangerous creatures too, such as scorpions and camel

18

spiders, but these are shy and rarely seen. Many birds spend the winter in the desert en route to other places but few nest there. Among the species which do nest is the grey shrike.

The greatest number and variety of birds are to be found around the coast, as this is where there is the most food. These include the rare sooty falcons and ospreys which nest on the almost uninhabited Hawar Islands to the south of Bahrain. Groups of beautiful pink flamingoes also come to spend their winters round the southern coasts.

In addition to other plant life, the Hawar Islands have many beautiful lichens growing on their rocks. Since lichens only grow in a clean atmosphere this shows how free from pollution these islands are.

The seas around Bahrain are not teeming with life as might be expected. There are two reasons for this: first, the sea is very salty; and secondly, the water has such a wide range of

An oyster being split open to reveal the pearl inside its shell. The seas around Bahrain provide ideal conditions for oysters

Waterbuck in Al-Areen Wildlife Park, an area in the south-west of Bahrain devoted to the preservation of Arabia's flora and fauna

temperatures. It is quite cool in the winter but in the summer it can feel like warm soup. These conditions are, however, good for oysters, on which Bahrain's wealth once depended, and for shrimps and other shellfish.

Strange, large sea creatures which also live in the waters around Bahrain are the dugongs. These are shy, rare animals and are thought to be the origin of the legends about mermaids, although they bear little resemblance to the beautiful mermaids in story-books. It is thought that the link between the dugong and the mermaid came about because the dugong holds its young to its teat with a flipper and in this way resembles a human mother. There are also turtles, dolphins and baracudas. Sharks

20

are rarely seen and there are no recent records of any shark attacks. Sea-snakes, which are potentially dangerous, can often be seen when the water becomes warm. These snakes have a very toxic venom which affects the nervous system. But the snakes are not normally aggressive and, luckily, they have extremely small mouths. This means that they can only get their jaws round the smallest pieces of flesh, such as the skin between the fingers.

Although man is encroaching on the habitat of the plants and animals in Bahrain (as is happening in most other parts of the world), there are still such untouched areas as the Hawar Islands, and schemes such as Al-Areen Wildlife Park for the preservation of the flora and fauna of Arabia.

Bahrain's History

The comparatively green islands of Bahrain, like many other places in the Middle East, have given rise to a number of stories connected with the Garden of Eden. This region was certainly the site of many ancient civilizations; the task of modern-day archaeologists is to examine the evidence and try to separate fact from fiction—story from reality.

Ancient flint tools have been found in the desert in the south-west of Bahrain. These have been identified as coming from Bahrain's Old Stone Age but can only be roughly dated. They are thought to be approximately 20,000 to 50,000 years old. Many more flints have been found in the central parts of the island. These have been more accurately dated between 8000 and 6000 B.C. and are thought to be between 10,000 and 8,000 years old. They include arrowheads used by nomadic hunters who originally moved from place to place to find food, and later developed more settled crop-farming using a sickle-shaped flint to till the soil. Similar tools have been found in Iraq and in India.

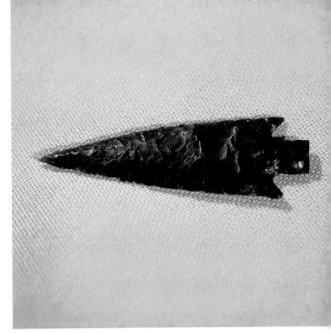

A flint arrowhead, found in the desert in the south-west of Bahrain and thought to be at least 20,000 years old

There is evidence that, by 3800 B.C., trading between Bahrain and neighbouring states had begun. Pottery fragments (called "shards" by archaeologists) have been excavated and identified as coming from potteries in southern Iraq, then known as Mesopotamia.

Although it may not have been the Garden of Eden, evidence of Bahrain being the fabled Land of Dilmun is more substantial. The Sumerians, who lived in Mesopotamia in about 2000 B.C., thought Dilmun was a kind of Holy Land or Paradise for heroes and wise men, where nobody ever died. For them, it was a land blessed by Enki, the God of Sweet Waters. On an old stone tablet found in Iraq, the Land of Dilmun is described as the place where "the croak of the raven was not heard, the bird of death did not utter a cry of death, the lion did not devour, the wolf

23

did not rend the lamb, the dove did not mourn, there was no widow, no sickness, no old age, no lamentation''. More factual writing about Dilmun tells of an island with abundant fresh water, lying some two days' sail with a following wind from Mesopotamia.

If this referred to Bahrain, and it clearly could, it seems strange that Dilmun, the land of immortality where no one ever died, is represented in Bahrain by one of the biggest cemeteries in the world. There are over 100,000 burial mounds dating from this time in the northern half of the island. Called *muraqib* by the local people, these mounds are dome-shaped and range from eight metres (twenty-six feet) to over twenty-four metres (eighty feet) in height and from over five metres (eighteen feet) to over thirty metres (one hundred feet) in diameter, depending on the importance of the occupant.

One of the many burial mounds of Dilmun, in the north of Bahrain — possibly an indication of how wealthy this ancient civilization was

Unlike ancient burials in Egypt and Mesopotamia, not only royalty but also quite ordinary people were given elaborate burials and a tomb of their own in Bahrain. The great number of mounds confirms that Dilmun must have been wealthy to afford such expensive funerals for so many. Perhaps this is the answer to the riddle; for, if everyone from royalty down could be provided with a burial mound in which they could be reborn, Dilmun really would be the land of the immortals—where common people as well as kings gained life after death.

The mounds are in the western region of Bahrain on land at least ten metres (thirty-three feet) above sea level. This allowed lower ground to be used for settlements, ensuring that villages had a constant supply of fresh spring water, whilst the graves were high enough to remain dry.

A city was built in the north of the main island of Bahrain near what is now Qalaat al-Bahrain (Bahrain Fort). This was the rich trading-centre of the State of Dilmun. Here, goods such as gold and ivory from the Indus Valley (now Pakistan) and copper from Oman were exchanged for woollen goods and pottery from Mesopotamia (now Iraq). Excavations of this city have uncovered pottery, glassware, jewellery, statues and seals. These seals were stones which had been used to stamp impressions in soft clay or wax in order to show the ownership of goods which were to be exchanged, much as a trademark or signature might be used today. Fifty of these seals have a circular design unique to Bahrain. They bear the impression of simple human and animal forms, and are thought to have come from

25

**The bronze bull's head
found at Barbar temple**

a stone-carver's workshop. Near by, at Diraz and Barbar, temples have been excavated. Within their walls, carvings and figures of animals have been found. These are thought to be connected with the rituals and religious ceremonies performed in the temples. Perhaps the finest is the bronze bull's head found at Barbar temple.

The Bahraini people are very proud of their ancient past. The designs of the Barbar bull's head and the Dilmun seals are well-known symbols of the Dilmun civilization. The name Dilmun itself, or the alternative spelling Delmon, now survives as a trade name; and is used, among other things, for a hotel, a poultry farm, a garage and a sports club.

From about 2000 B.C. the importance of Dilmun as a trading centre began to decline, since the cities of the Indus Valley (in

26

modern Pakistan) were destroyed by invading tribes and the Sumerians lost control in Mesopotamia (now Iraq). Wealth returned, however, in about 700 B.C. when the surrounding countries became settled enough to resume trading. Bahrain was next controlled by a number of different rulers: the Babylonians (Assyrians) of the Mesopotamian Empire (600 B.C.), the Persians from what is now Iran (540 B.C.), the Greeks under Alexander the Great and his successors, who noted that Bahrain, or "Tylos" as they called it, was already famous for its pearls (300 B.C. to A.D. 300), Arab tribes (A.D. 300 to 400) and the Persians again (A.D. 400 to 600).

One of the most important events in Bahrain's history was the coming of Islam in the seventh century A.D. For the next three hundred and fifty years, Bahrain was ruled by governors on behalf of the Caliphs (rulers) of Damascus (Syria) and Baghdad (Iraq). There followed a rather uncertain period when Bahrain changed hands many times as the Persians and the Arab states on the mainland competed for its control.

In 1521, Bahrain was captured by the Portuguese who wanted to gain control of the rich spice trade between India and Europe—previously handled by the Arabs. The following year the Portuguese built the Bahrain Fort (Qalaat al-Bahrain) which survives to this day on the site of the ancient city of Dilmun.

Bahrain remained under the protection of the Portuguese until 1602 when the Portuguese governor murdered a wealthy Bahraini in order to gain possession of his famous pearl collection. The murdered man's brother then killed the governor

27

and, with the help of the people, captured the fort and put Bahrain under the protection of the Persians once again. A period of piracy and local wars followed, with Bahrain falling into the hands of the Omanis and being bought back by the Persians for a large sum of money.

The last successful invasion of Bahrain was carried out by the family of the present ruler of Bahrain more than two hundred years ago. The Al-Khalifas were an important merchant family who originated in Kuwait. They moved to Qatar to be nearer the pearl industry in Bahrain. They built a fort and a large town at Zubara in Qatar. The Persians, who controlled Bahrain, felt threatened and so attacked Zubara in 1783. The Al-Khalifas fought off the attack and, with the help of the Kuwaiti fleet, drove the Persians out of Bahrain. It took Sheikh Ahmed al-Fatih (the conqueror) several years to establish Al-Khalifa rule—during which time the Omanis and the Wahabi tribe from the Arabian mainland each captured Bahrain and ruled for some time.

In 1861, Sheikh Muhammad Al-Khalifa signed a "Perpetual Treaty of Peace and Friendship" with the British. This treaty was concerned with stopping pirate ships and slave traders using the islands, in return for trade and protection from the British. Although there were many disputes involving exile, imprisonment and death within the ruling Al-Khalifa family and threats of attacks from Persia, Turkey and the Arab tribes, the presence of British warships in the Gulf managed to preserve the stability of Bahrain. Eight years later, the first Sheikh Isa

The country palace at Sakhir, where Sheik Hamad died in 1942. The palace remains locked and shuttered to this very day, as a mark of respect for the late Bahraini ruler

came to power. He became the island's longest-reigning ruler: he served his country for fifty-four years.

The twentieth century brought sudden and dramatic changes to Bahrain. In 1932, Sheikh Isa the First died, and his son Sheikh Hamad, the heir apparent (next in line), was appointed ruler of Bahrain. This was also the year in which oil was struck at Well Number One near Jebel Dukhan, in which the first Imperial Airways aircraft landed at Bahrain on the way to India, and in which the Bahrain telephone service was started. Three years later work started on the Bahrain Petroleum Company (BAPCO) Refinery, and oil revenue (money earned from the petroleum industry) was channelled into the country's education

29

and health services. In 1942, the causeway between Muharraq and Manama was completed. During this year, too, Sheikh Hamad died at his country palace at Sakhir—which remains locked and shuttered, as a mark of respect, to this day. He was succeeded by Sheikh Sulman, the present ruler's father, who continued to develop social and economic advancement. In 1958, a friendly pact concerning oil income was made with Saudi Arabia and about this time the British began to decrease their involvement in affairs of state.

Sheikh Isa bin Sulman Al-Khalifa became the present ruler (and tenth member of the family to rule Bahrain) on December 16, 1961. This day is now commemorated every year as National

The docks at Mina Sulman, Bahrain's deep-water port

Day—a holiday for everyone, with traditional singing and dancing in the parks and a grand firework display. The Sheikh also invites well-wishers to come and meet him at his *Majlis* (reception) in West Rifaa.

During the first ten years of Sheikh Isa's reign, the Bahraini *dinar* was introduced to replace the Indian *rupee* which had previously been the unit of currency, the deep-water port for large ships was opened—named Mina Sulman after the previous ruler—and Isa Town was completed, to house Bahraini citizens.

Sheikh Isa formally declared Bahrain to be an independent sovereign state on August 14, 1971. The following day a new treaty of friendship was signed between Bahrain and Britain. Later that year, Bahrain was admitted to the United Nations as the 128th member. Once again, Bahrain is a state with a voice to be listened to in the world community. For such a small nation, it has a remarkably realistic independent identity.

The People of Bahrain

The people of Bahrain—the Bahrainis—are mainly of Arab and Iranian descent. The Arabs who originally came from the mainland of Arabia have a strong sense of identity and their surnames often give a clue to their origins. For example, the name Wahabi comes originally from one of the tribes of Saudi Arabia. Several generations ago many Iranians came to settle in Bahrain since, at one time in its history, Bahrain was ruled by Iran, then known as Persia.

Today, Bahrainis make up about eighty per cent of the population. The other twenty per cent are temporary workers. Bahrain, like other Gulf states and developing countries, has more jobs than people to do them, particularly in certain complicated and skilled areas of work. These temporary workers are called expatriates. They cannot live in Bahrain permanently, and can only stay as long as they have a job. There are expatriates from nearly every country in the world, but most are Arabs from other neighbouring states, Indians, Pakistanis

32

and people from South-East Asia, Japan, Europe and America.

The 1981 census showed that in forty years the population of Bahrain had grown from 89,970 to 350,798. The present population is thought to be about 430,000 (about the same number of people as in the city of Bristol in England). However, in Bahrain the majority of the population is young—fifty-four per cent are under twenty years old.

The people of Bahrain are among the most sophisticated in the Gulf. Being a trading nation, it has always had a lot of contact with people and ideas from other countries. Women in Bahrain have more freedom than in most neighbouring states. Very few young women wear the veil, many drive and have responsible, well-paid jobs. Fifteen per cent of the work-force is female. Many women still wear the traditional *abba*—a thin black cloak which protects their clothes from dust—but underneath they often wear the latest European or American fashions adapted to suit local taste (with long sleeves and knee-length skirts). Village women often wear traditional dress, a *thobe* (long dress) over baggy trousers. Traditional dress is often worn both in town and country on important occasions, such as weddings. The women then wear beautifully embroidered *thobes*, and gold jewellery, and paint their hands and feet with intricate designs in henna (a reddish-brown dye).

The local climate and religion have led to the development of the distinctive national dress which is still worn by many Bahraini men, especially in summer when it helps to keep the wearer cool. A long tunic *(thobe)* is worn (usually white in the

Bahraini men in their distinctive national dress — the *thobe* (long white tunic) and *guttra* (head-dress)

summer but it may be grey and made of thicker material in the winter). The head-dress for men is a white or coloured cloth, a *guttra,* held in place by an *agaal.* The *agaal* is made of black cord. In some parts of Arabia the cord is said to have been made of camel hair and to have been used to tie camels' legs at night to stop them wandering. This dress is cool and protects the

34

wearer from the strong sun. When the weather is less hot a *bisht* is worn as well. This is a thin cloak of black or brown, often edged in gold thread.

Life in Bahrain is dominated by the religion of Islam, although other religions are tolerated. Its teachings permeate every aspect of life—dress, food, marriage, etc. Muslims (adherents of Islam) are followers of the prophet Muhammad who lived in Saudi Arabia over 1,400 years ago. After his death, his teachings were written down in the *Quran,* the holy book of Islam. Just as Christianity has different followers believing slightly different things, so does Islam. In Christianity there are Protestants and Roman Catholics (among the many different denominations). So it is with Islam. In Bahrain there are two groups of Muslims: the Sunni and the Shia. They both follow the prophet Muhammad but believe in slightly different things.

For all Muslims the day begins with early prayers when the *Muezzin* (prayer-caller) calls from the mosque (the Muslim place of worship). Nowadays, nearly all the mosques have loudspeakers by which the voice of the *Muezzin* is broadcast. During the day there are four more prayers. Only the men pray in the mosques, the women pray at home. If it is not possible to visit the mosque for prayer, men unroll a prayer mat at work, in the garden or in any convenient place. Muslims can now buy special watches which tell the times of prayer and the direction of Mecca. (All Muslims should face Mecca, their holy city in Saudi Arabia, when they pray.)

Like other religions, Islam has special festivals which celebrate

The Barbar village mosque (place of worship), with its golden dome and slender minarets

both sad and happy events. These do not fall at the same time each year because the Muslim Calendar is different from the Western or Gregorian Calendar. The Muslim year is based on the phases of the moon and has thirteen months. The years are counted from the time of Muhammad. The Muslim Calendar is 580 years behind the Western Calendar which is used in daily business affairs.

The main festivals are Ramadan, Eid Al Adha, Ashoora and the Prophet's Birthday. Ramadan is a month of fasting. During this month, Muslims should not eat between sunrise and sunset, and people of other religions are not allowed to eat in public. Strict Muslims do not even swallow their own saliva, so when

36

Ramadan falls in summer, the hottest part of the year, it can be a very difficult time for people working outside. The evenings are spent feasting and visiting friends and family. At the end of Ramadan is the festival of Eid Al Fitr, when families give presents to each other and people give money to charity.

Most Muslims would like to make a pilgrimage to their holy city of Mecca at least once during their lifetime. This journey can be undertaken at any time but there is a special season for the pilgrimage when events in the prophet's life are remembered, which is called the Haj. During the Haj, animals (sheep) are traditionally killed and the meat is given to the poor. Nowadays, some of the meat is sent to poor countries and given to hungry people. At the end of the Haj is the festival of Eid Al Adha. The Prophet's Birthday is another occasion for celebration.

The saddest event in the Muslim calendar is Ashoora. This commemorates a great battle and the death of one of the leaders of the Shia Muslims. At this time, some of the Shias march in procession beating themselves and cutting themselves with blades. This is to show how sorry they are for what happened in the past. At this time many of the Shia Muslims, especially the women, wear mourning colours: black and white.

Traditional food is often eaten at times of Eids (holidays). This is based on fish, rice, meat and dates. (Pork is not eaten, as it is forbidden by Islam.) The best-known traditional dish of Bahrain is *machbous*—fish or meat served with rice. *Muhammar* is brown sweet rice served with sugar or dates. Delicious snacks can be bought in the *souk* (market): small fried potato-cakes, and crispy pastry-cases filled with meat or cheese or sugar and nuts; these are called *sambousas*. Another sweet sold in the *souk* is *halwa*—a kind of green sticky sweet filled with spices and nuts. Bahrain also has many modern supermarkets which supply food from most areas of the world: steak from Australia, noodles from China, cheese from France, fresh salmon from Scotland. It is possible to buy almost any kind of food, either in a shop or restaurant, but as it has to be imported it is usually quite expensive.

Although Bahrain still retains many of its traditions, it has changed into a modern Middle-Eastern state. These changes are reflected in modern family life. A Muslim is allowed four wives but nowadays most young men have only one wife. The husband and wife have usually met before the wedding. They

Muslims at prayer. All Muslims must face Mecca, their holy city in Saudi Arabia, when they pray

Bahrainis celebrating the festival of Eid Al Fitr, held at the end of Ramadan (the Muslim month of fasting)

may be cousins or they may have met at work or college. In the past, the bride and groom often had not seen each other, as the wedding was arranged by the parents. The bride might have been only twelve or thirteen years old. Now girls have often completed their education and have jobs of their own by the time they get married.

A sum of money is paid to the bride by the groom when they marry. This is usually decided by the families involved and can be quite a large amount. The bride may keep this money for herself, but often the couple use it to buy things for the home.

39

Weddings are often lavish affairs. If they are in a village, the whole village will probably be invited. If they are in town, there may be as many as five or six hundred guests. Traditionally, the wedding party is split into two groups. There is one celebration for men and a separate one for women. Sometimes the parties take place in two different hotels. Sometimes, wedding parties are mixed. The wedding may take up to three days, including sumptuous meals for family and friends, a religious ceremony and a henna party for the women. (At a henna party, the women decorate the hands and feet of the bride with intricate patterns painted on with henna—a reddish-brown paste.)

In contrast to this, divorce is quick. The husband has only

to say: "I divorce you" three times. If the wife wants a divorce, it is a more complicated affair.

After the wedding, couples used to live with the groom's family. The wife would keep her own name but live as part of her husband's household. Now, many young couples choose to live separately from their parents in their own apartments or houses. However, as Bahrain is such a small place, they will still be close to their families and most grandparents and relatives have a share in looking after the young children.

In Bahrain, death is not marked by any great ceremony and there are no elaborate gravestones. Burial, facing Mecca, is swift. If an important person dies his house may be shut up for some time after the death.

Life in the Towns and Villages

Bahrain has four towns: two are old and two are new. Muharraq is the oldest. It is on the separate island of Muharraq which is joined to the mainland by a causeway. Muharraq used to be the capital of Bahrain, and the first Sheikh Isa had a palace there. At that time, the palaces of the sheikhs (rulers) were the only buildings more than one storey high. Nobody else was allowed to build two-storey buildings, as these would overlook the palaces of the sheikhs. A great deal of the life of the household used to take place on the flat roofs of the houses; children would play there, and their parents would relax there. In the summer, the whole family would sleep on the roof as it was the coolest place to be. Now there is air-conditioning, most people sleep indoors, especially when it is very hot. In the old areas of Muharraq, round the old *souk*, some of the traditional houses of Bahrain can still be seen. They were built to be as cool as possible in the hot weather. They are close together and, in the *souk* area, palm branches and lengths of material are stretched across the

42

narrow lanes to provide extra shade. The lanes are just wide enough to allow donkeys to pass through them.

One or two houses with wind-towers still remain, though many of the older houses are being pulled down. Wind-towers provided a form of air-conditioning. They were tall towers open on all four sides at the top so that they could catch the wind, whichever direction it was blowing from. The wind was channelled down the tower and was cooled on its way down by passing between pieces of wet cloth which were hung over poles in its path. This heavier, cool air circulated round the house as the hot air rose. The ceilings of the old houses were high, and this too helped to keep the house cool.

It is very difficult to see inside these old houses. They have large locked gates and small windows which are shuttered or barred. And the garden is on the inside of the house in a courtyard. Arabs like to be private, and to shut out the outside world when they are at home. But they do like to know what is going on too! In the past, when they led a restricted life, the women would watch what was going on in the street below from a shuttered balcony. Some of these balconies can still be seen in older parts of the town, as can fanlights made of coloured glass, which are a distinctive feature of Arab architecture.

The Bahraini government is trying to preserve the few old houses left which were built with coral stones from the sea and which are supposed to be very cool. One of these is the Sayadi House. This house belonged to a pearl-merchant of Muharraq. In it there is a room with no windows where the merchant could count his money without being overlooked. It also has a *majlis*—a large meeting-room for men.

Apart from the fascinating old *souk* and the nearby houses, there is also an ancient fort guarding the entrance to Muharraq. It is a reminder of past battles. This is Arad Fort, originally built by the Portuguese and later used by the Omanis at a time when there were pirates in the Gulf.

The old part of Muharraq is surrounded by the new. As well as a new market, there are many beautiful modern houses and a modern airport which is the busiest in the Gulf.

Muharraq used to be the main pearling centre, and there are still many *dhows* (Arab boats) tied up round the coast. These can be hired for trips to other islands. Bahrainis and expatriates like to spend Friday (their weekend) on the water—fishing, diving and swimming. During the week, the *dhows* are used for fishing and for carrying cargo up and down the Gulf.

Arad fort, originally built by the Portuguese

Manama—the name means "sleeping-place"—is the other old town of Bahrain. It is now the capital. The land area of Manama has greatly increased over recent years. This is because much land has been reclaimed from the sea. The sea-bed has been dredged to make deep channels to enable ships to pass through more easily. And what was once part of the sea-bed now has modern hotels and offices standing on it. As it is the capital, there are many embassies in Manama, as well as offices, hotels and government buildings. These stand on wide modern roads lined with trees and flowers.

The heart of Manama is its large busy *souk*. The roads are narrow and crowded. They are frequently being dug up to repair old sewage and electrical systems. The *souk* is divided into distinct areas, all adjoining each other. The main road is the Bab Al Bahrain—"the Gate of Bahrain". On this street, shops sell electrical goods, television sets, the latest stereo equipment, refrigerators, washing-machines, etc. Further on, is the cloth *souk* where all kinds of fabrics hang from the stalls. There are also many tailors. They do not work from patterns but they will copy a dress or suit from a magazine picture. Next is the gold *souk*. Here there are small shops filled with gold jewellery of every kind. The shopkeepers do not seem worried about their gold being stolen. Goldsmiths sit out in the street melting gold to make into jewellery. The gold *souk* is usually filled with women shopping for gold. Traditionally, it is their chief form of wealth and, rather than keep money in a bank, they prefer to use it to buy gold.

Manama, the capital of Bahrain—the city that has expanded dramatically in recent years owing to an ambitious programme to reclaim land from the sea

The sound of hammering and banging comes from the blacksmiths' *souk*. Trunks, pots and pans are all made here from aluminium. Anything metal can be made here. The dirty open workshops and roaring fires look like story-book pictures of devils' workshops. The plumbers' part of the *souk* is next, full of pipes, sinks, toilets and tiles. Next to it is the car *souk*. It has many small garages where people are busy repairing and welding.

A quiet corner away from all the noise is the street of shops full of herbs and spices. Most of the ''shops'' do not have glass

46

shop-windows; instead, they open straight onto the street. Here there are sacks full of coriander, cumin and chillies, all used in making curries; and great sacks of huge tobacco leaves. In between the shops are small cafés where men sit and drink coffee and smoke hubble-bubble water pipes.

On Wednesdays and Fridays, village people bring in goods to sell. They brings such things as parrots, embroidered *thobes,* baskets and mats.

Fruit, vegetables, meat and fish are no longer sold in the *souk.* Instead, these foods are sold in the new central market. This is a huge covered market, rather like an aircraft hangar, where fresh foodstuffs of all descriptions are sold under more hygienic,

**Part of the market in
Manama**

controlled conditions. The exhibition centre is also part of this complex. Businessmen come here from all over the Gulf to view the latest developments in their field. They stay in the new hotels and relax in the luxurious surroundings.

Manama is soon to have a new museum, theatre and mosque. Its present museum has become too small and, although there are many mosques in Bahrain, there is not really a national mosque. Bahrain is trying to keep what is best of the past and combine it with what is best of the present.

Ten kilometres (six miles) from Manama on the eastern side of the island is Isa Town. This town, which has more than twenty-one thousand inhabitants, was specially designed as a ''new town'' and was opened in 1968. It has a swimming-pool, a sports stadium, shops, mosques and a health centre. It is still being expanded and some of the original houses now look quite old. This is because the climate in Bahrain is very harsh so that buildings soon look shabby. The temperature ranges from quite low to extremely high. The atmosphere is also very humid and very salty. All these factors combine and mean that buildings soon look old, even when they have only been up for a few years.

The latest ''new town'' to be opened in Bahrain is Hamad Town. It is named after the present ruler's eldest son, Sheikh Hamad. Hamad Town was officially opened in 1984 and some families have now moved into their new homes. All the houses have been specially designed to reflect modern Arab architecture. The town is on the western side of the island and the gleaming white houses can be seen from quite a distance. Part of the town

Some of the gleaming white buildings of Hamad Town, named after Sheik Hamad, the heir to the Bahraini throne

has been built around the ancient burial-mounds of Dilmun and these have been incorporated into the design. Hamad Town has all the facilities of a modern town: shops, schools, parks, health centres and a museum. Eventually, it will house eighty thousand people.

Both Isa Town and Hamad Town have been built on what were quite dry areas of Bahrain. The water for these towns comes from large desalination plants (which extract the salt from sea-water), as does most of the mains piped water supply. The older towns and villages grew up where there were *ains*—springs of fresh water. These *ains* are still very important to village life. They provide water for agriculture but they cannot supply enough water for everyone.

49

**Threshing coriander
seeds—a fragrant
spice grown
in Bahrain**

Most of the villages are in agricultural areas and are surrounded by date gardens which are really small farms. The fields are very small and they are divided up by irrigation channels. The water for the date gardens used to be raised out of the wells by donkeys turning a water-wheel but now diesel engines are used. In the past, Bahrain produced enough fruit, dates and vegetables for most of its own needs and if there was a surplus it was exported. When oil was discovered, many of the village people left the hard life of working in the date gardens and went to work for the oil company and in other industries. Many of the date gardens were neglected, and the increase in population meant that houses were built on land that was once farmed. As a result, Bahrain began importing more food. The

50

government is trying to encourage farming to provide more local food and keep the island cool and green. (Trees help to keep the temperature down and to give shade.) Now new date gardens are being planted, and some villagers commute to work in the towns during the day and then work on their land in the evenings.

At Budaiya, the village in the north-west corner of the island, there is a government experimental farm which tries to find the best crops to grow in Bahrain's climate. There are also two herds of Friesian cows on the island. They were imported to give fresh milk. The local cows, which have humps behind their heads like the cows in India, do not give much milk. Many village people also keep goats which wander about, looking for scraps of food.

Friesian cows, specially imported to provide fresh milk

Water is vital for agriculture. In addition, Bahrain has one of the highest water-consumption rates per person in the world and the government is trying very hard to educate people not to waste water. Before people had taps in their houses they would either go and fetch water from the *ains*—this was usually the woman's job—or buy it from a water-seller who brought it in a bag made of camel-skin. Although most houses now have piped water, in some areas it is not suitable for drinking so drinking-water must be bought. This is called "sweet water" to distinguish it from the tap-water which has a salty taste. The water-sellers nowadays bring drinking-water to the door, not in camel-skins but in large plastic jerricans which they fill from a water-tanker. Today, in Bahrain, the remains of an ancient system of irrigation can still be seen. These are *gnats*. The *gnats* are systems of underground tunnels which carried water from an area with water to a dry area. The water was sent underground to prevent it evaporating in the hot weather.

Nowadays, most of the villages have electricity and running water, a school and a health centre. The people are not isolated from the towns; there are tarmac roads connecting all the villages to the main roads, and quite frequent bus services. Most houses in the villages are now built of modern materials and there are very few *barastis*—houses made of palm branches.

In the past, the palm tree supplied most of the needs of the people and every part of the tree was used. "The palm will look after you if you look after the palm" was the theory. The palm requires a lot of care if it is to grow well and give a lot of dates.

52

A typical Bahraini village—most houses are now built of modern materials rather than the more traditional palm branches

The dates, which are a very good source of nourishment, are delicious either fresh or dried. Now they are also being frozen to make them more readily available out of season. The dates which are not of such good quality are fed to animals. The thin springy branches among which the dates grow can be used as brooms; and the flexible stems can be woven into baskets for carrying chickens. Palm leaves may also be woven to make baskets, mats and fans. These can be bought in the *souk* where the local people come to sell their goods on Wednesdays and Fridays. In the past, the fibre which grows at the top of the palm tree and looks like brown matting was used to make ropes and as a "pan-scrub" for cleaning pots and pans. The lumps of wood at the thick end of the palm branches were often used to make fires for cooking, before gas- and electric-stoves became

53

Alfalfa growing in the shade of date palms

widespread. The branches were also used for making fish-traps which can still be seen in the shallow waters around Bahrain. Even cradles for babies were once made from palm branches. The trunk of the tree has always been used for building purposes. And palm leaves and coloured lights are a sure sign that there is to be a celebration. Palm fronds are used to decorate the house when there is a wedding. Finally, after the hard work of the date garden, the juice of the dates mixed with water makes a most refreshing drink. Village life has always depended on the date palm. In addition, crops such as tomatoes, carrots and cabbages, grapes, pomegranates and alfalfa (for feeding animals) all benefit from the shade that it provides.

54

Traditional Crafts

Although Bahrain now has modern industries, traditional crafts have not been completely abandoned. It is possible to see boats being made and cloth being woven in the same way as it was done centuries ago. Most of the crafts centre round the villages; and particular villages are well-known for certain crafts.

Dhow-building does not form a major craft in any one village but takes place along the shore. The *dhows* are still made in the original way, without using metal nails, and to a traditional design, but diesel engines have replaced the more picturesque sails. There are many different kinds of *dhow*. They are used to carry people and cargo up and down the Arabian Gulf, and also for fishing and pearling, although there are only two pearling-*dhows* working now. The Arabs who live by the sea have a reputation for being fine sailors. Historic battles in the Gulf often depended on fast ships and good seamanship.

The *dhows* are made of wood imported from India. Boat-builders using traditional tools can still be seen at the *dhow-*

One of the many types of *dhow* which are still used in the Arabian Gulf. This one has a traditional picturesque sail rather than the diesel engine more commonly used today

builders yard near central market. This is not their traditional site but, as more land is reclaimed, they have to move to be near the sea. In fact, *dhows* are sometimes left stranded high and dry before they are even put in the water. This is because the time it takes for a *dhow* to be built in the traditional manner is far outstripped by the speed with which modern methods reclaim land from the sea. A *dhow* may be started on the shoreline but by the time it is completed it could be far from the sea, perhaps even separated from it by a new major road, and so require rollers and cranes to transport it to the sea for launching.

Next to the *dhow*-builders yards are heaps of large wire cages

56

big enough to sit in. These are fish-traps which are taken out to sea and left to catch all kinds of fish. Another kind of fish-trap is made out of palm branches stuck into the sea-bed in shallow water. The principle is the same in both cases: the fish are funnelled into the narrow entrance to the trap but, once inside, find nothing to guide them back to the narrow opening again.

Anyone who visits a shop or office in Bahrain and does business with an Arab may be offered a cup of their traditional tea or coffee. Nowadays, it is often kept in a vacuum flask but you may be lucky enough to be offered coffee from a traditional pot. The coffee-pots are no longer made in Bahrain but, nevertheless, they are very much a part of the Bahraini tradition

**Building *dhows* using
traditional tools**

Repairing a fish-trap made from palm branches

of hospitality. Coffee-pots are made to be heated in the embers of a fire; they are made of brass or copper, and have a long curved spout. Many are sold as souvenirs of the island.

Bahraini pottery is made at A'ali village. It is beige, unglazed pottery made of local clay and is quite rough in appearance. The potters also make pots for hubble-bubble pipes. Smoked at coffee-shops in the *souk*, these are long twisty pipes attached to a pot of water through which the smoke is bubbled to cool it. The potters make plant pots, water-jars and children's money-boxes, although crockery for everyday use is imported. A'ali village is surrounded by the ancient burial-mounds of Dilmun and these are used as kilns. The inside of the mound is hollowed out, the pottery is put in and then wood is used to heat the ''kiln'' so that the pottery is hardened. Lime is also made in these kilns. Lime stones are first heated in the kilns and then beaten into a white powder to make whitewash.

Before modern medicine came to Bahrain the people relied on herbal medicines. These were made from palm tree flowers, pollen, buds and imported herbs. Some of them are still used, especially in country districts. The village most noted for this is Jidhaffs.

Near Jidhaffs is a village named Sanabis, known for the embroidery done by the women there. They sew beautiful designs onto their national costume—the long dress called a *thobe*. The embroidery is often in gold and can be very complicated.

Pottery being made at A'ali village

They also embroider the cloaks called *bisht* which are worn by men. They sell the cloaks and dresses at the Wednesday market in the *souk*.

Further down the road from the embroiderers are the fabric-weavers of Bani Jamra. They weave the black cloth for the traditional *abba* or *abbaya* which many of the women wear. Of course the thirteen weavers in the village cannot supply all of Bahrain and much fine, silky material is imported. The cloth woven at Bani Jamra is slightly thicker. It can be seen stretched out to dry outside the weavers' houses.

On the other side of the island, near the sea, is the village of Sitra. Here are made mats which can be found in many mosques and homes. These mats are not made from rushes but from a kind of grass called *aseel* which grows between the sweet water of the land and the salt water of the sea.

One of the fabric weavers of Bani Jamra

The government of Bahrain is encouraging the survival of traditional crafts as a way of keeping the nation's customs alive and also as a means of promoting tourism. Many village women who have had little education are being persuaded to take up craftwork in order to supplement the income of their family. This also means that they can meet other women and hear about modern child-care at the village centres where they go to learn new skills. Examples of many traditional crafts are on show at the Bahrain Museum and the National Heritage Centre.

Industries Old and New

In recent years, Bahrain has developed a number of modern industries with the money earned as a result of its oil discoveries. Before oil, Bahrain was dependent on the pearling industry for revenue. Although it was more prosperous than some of its neighbours, Bahrain used to be quite a poor nation without much significance to the rest of the world.

The early years of this century saw the pearling industry reach its peak and then steadily decline.

Pearls, according to the *Quran,* the holy book of Islam, were the property of paradise. And, since ancient times, the pearls of the Arabian Gulf have had the reputation of being the finest in the world. It is said that this is because of the mixture of salt water and fresh water in the seas around Bahrain. A great price was often paid for the pearls in terms of human hardship. The lives of the divers who dived for the pearls was difficult and often dangerous.

The methods of pearling remained the same for hundreds of

years. Modern diving equipment, such as diving-suits and oxygen, was originally forbidden by law. This was to give everyone an equal chance of finding the best pearls, without the richer merchants (who could afford expensive equipment) gaining an unfair advantage. As the best pearls were thought to be found in the deepest water, this made the diver's job all the more dangerous.

The pearling season, called *Al Ghaws,* lasted four months from June to October—the hottest months of the year. The traditional wooden boats which were used were a kind of *dhow* called a *sambuk.* The crew of the *sambuk* numbered about sixty, including divers, pullers who pulled up the divers and rowed the boat when

A pearling *dhow*, or *sambuk*

Oysters being pulled up
to the *dhow* after the
pearl-diver has
completed his dive

there was not enough wind to make use of the sails (there were few engines in those days), a couple of ship's boys, a cook, the captain's mate and the captain. When they were working, the divers wore nothing except for a pair of dark-coloured shorts; any bright-coloured clothing might have attracted dangerous fish. In the jelly-fish season they wore thin cotton garments to avoid being stung.

Each diver had two ropes: One was weighted with a stone and was used to descend quickly to the sea-bed. The other was fastened to the bag used to collect the oyster-shells in which the pearls were found. The oyster-shell is in two halves and is anchored to the sea-bed by a strong thread. It is often quite difficult to remove. The divers also wore leather guards on their

64

fingers to protect them. The rough scaly appearance of the outside of the oyster contrasts with the beautiful inner shell, which is shiny and irridescent. If the inside of the oyster is damaged, or if some grit or dirt gets inside the shell, then the oyster secretes more of the substance that makes the beautiful shell lining. This substance covers the injured part and forms a pearl. So not every oyster contains a pearl.

As well as having guards on his fingers, the diver also wore leather guards on his toes to protect him from the sharp coral. The diver made ten dives and then had a rest. It was a very exhausting job. When all the divers had surfaced from a dive, the pullers hauled up the bags filled with shells and emptied them on the deck. This was accompanied by a great deal of stamping and clapping. There were also many pearling songs, but most of them have now been forgotten.

In the late afternoon, when the diving was finished, the divers would gather round the oysters and open them with their special pearling knives which had strong, curved blades. All the pearls were handed to the captain. After all the shells had been checked, the oysters were not eaten but thrown back into the sea. It was believed that this enriched the oyster-beds for the next season. It was now time for the divers to eat. Throughout the day, they would drink only a little coffee. The fresh water they needed would be collected from springs of water on the sea-bed.

The pearl merchants from Manama and Muharraq would go out to the pearling-boats in their luxurious launches and bargain with the captains to buy the pearls. The divers were

Pearls — the major source of Bahrain's wealth for many years

not paid wages but shared in the profits made from the sale of the pearls. Before they went to sea, the divers were paid money in advance so that their families would have something to spend while they were away. This meant that, if the money from the pearls was not enough to cover the advance, then the diver would have to work for the captain for the following seasons until his debt was paid off. So, for the divers pearling often brought little reward.

Pearling began to decline during the 1920s and 1930s. There were two reasons for this. One was the world recession; people did not have enough money to spend on luxury goods. The other was the development of cultured pearls by the Japanese. These pearls were ''grown'' in special pearl-beds. The growing of the pearls inside the oysters was carefully controlled and the shape of the pearls was therefore more regular.

66

Just when the pearling trade declined, the most important event in Bahrain's recent history occurred—the discovery of oil. Major Frank Holmes, a mining engineer from New Zealand, visited Bahrain in the 1920s. He was sure oil could be found. He had seen bitumen (a kind of tar which is found with oil) seeping up through the sand and he felt sure there was oil underneath. But in the 1920s Bahrain was more interested in discovering new sources of water than in discovering oil. So Frank Holmes agreed to drill water-wells and the government agreed, if they were successful, to allow him to drill for oil. The new water-wells were successful and so the Bahrain Petroleum Company (BAPCO) was formed in 1929.

In 1930, a geologist named Fred Davis walked round the rim rock of the Jebel Dhukhan—the hill in the centre of the island. After closely studying the ground, he decided on the site

One of Bahrain's earliest oil-wells, dating from the 1930s. Since then, oil has brought great wealth to the countries of the Arabian Gulf

of the first well. A drilling party arrived in May 1931 and, at six o' clock in the morning on June 1, 1932, oil began to flow. This was the first oil to be discovered in the Arabian Gulf region. Edward Skinner, who was in charge of the drilling party, described it as a ''real driller's dream''. Oil flowed at the rate of 9,600 barrels a day.

The Bahrain oilfield is a small one but, as it was discovered early, the wealth it brought allowed Bahrain to begin its rapid development sooner than its neighbours. A permanent camp was built near the first oil-wells and this later became the town of Awali, where many BAPCO employees live. The first cargo of crude oil was loaded from Sitra in 1934. (Crude oil is oil that has not been refined into a useable form such as petrol.)

In 1935, work began on the oil refinery which can now refine 255,000 barrels of crude oil a day. Not all the oil refined at the refinery comes from Bahrain—Bahrain does not produce enough oil. As Bahrain does not want to use up all its remaining oil too quickly, it imports more than three-quarters of the oil it refines from Saudi Arabia. This oil comes to Bahrain through a pipeline which is eighty-eight kilometres (fifty-five miles) long. After passing under the sea, it arrives on the west of the island just north of the Saudi Arabian Causeway. The pipeline then zigzags across the desert to the refinery at Sitra Industrial Complex on the east coast. The zigzags are important to allow for expansion during the high temperatures of the summer. For the same reason, the pipes are not fixed, but on rollers.

Although Bahrain's oil reserves are gradually being depleted,

The BAPCO (Bahrain Petroleum Company) oil refinery, capable of refining 255,000 barrels of crude oil per day

another source of energy often found with oil is being exploited to provide cheap energy. This source of energy is gas. It is thought that the known existing gas reserves will last for about another forty-five years, but exploration is already taking place to find new gas-fields. The gas is used to provide energy for the oil refinery and the aluminium smelter and to generate electricity. This cheap source of energy and the money from oil has been used for two purposes: to expand the welfare programme and to develop Bahrain's industry.

Bahrain soon realized that its oil would not last for ever and that it would need to establish other industries. These would ensure that people would have jobs when there was no more oil or if the country's income from oil were to drop, along with world oil prices. To safeguard its future, Bahrain has developed both service industries and manufacturing industries.

Service industries do not make anything; they sell their services. In the case of Bahrain, they provide services for their neighbours, the surrounding Gulf states, and also for countries further afield. Bahrain is a pleasant and reasonably efficient place in which to do business and to invest money made from oil. (Many of Bahrain's neighbours have large oil incomes.) Bahrain has become successful as a business centre for a number of reasons. It has good communications and is linked to Arabsat— the satellite launched jointly by Arab countries. Bahrain also had the first airport and telephone service in the Gulf. The country has a relaxed atmosphere and there are fewer restrictions on foreigners, both men and women, than there are in neighbouring states. This encourages many foreign companies to do business from Bahrain, as most expatriates and their wives and families enjoy living in Bahrain. The local population are often well-qualified to work in both foreign and local companies because they have had a long tradition of education. The main service industries are communications, hotels and banking. BATELCO, the Bahrain telephone company, provides direct telephone dialling to most countries in the world, as well as telex services. These are vital for a modern banking industry.

The hotel industry has many first-class hotels catering for visitors who come either for business or pleasure. They are usually full when there is an exhibition being held in Bahrain. These exhibitions cover a wide range of subjects; for example, computers, oil, education, books, food, etc. In order to train local people in the hotel industry, Bahrain has a Hotel and Catering College.

Banking is the most important of the service industries in Bahrain but it could not work efficiently without the support of the other service industries. Bahrain is also important as it is halfway between Hong Kong and London. When the financial centre of Hong Kong is closing, the financial centre of London is opening, because of the time differences around the world. Bahrain time falls in between those of the two centres. Another reason why Bahrain has become an important banking centre

The National Bank of Bahrain. Bahrain is now an important financial centre, with many companies choosing to bank there

is that the war in Lebanon has disrupted what used to be the banking centre of the Middle East. Now people leave their money in Bahrain because they find it easy to do business there. Most of the banks in Bahrain are called "offshore" banks. This does not mean that they are located in the sea but that they do not do business with individual people, only with companies. The offshore banks have to pay for a licence to operate in Bahrain, so the Bahrain government makes money from the banks.

Manufacturing industries in Bahrain have been financed with money from oil. The main heavy industries are aluminium-manufacture, ship-repairing and iron-pelletizing (making iron pellets). Bauxite, the material from which aluminium is made, is imported and so is the iron ore for the iron plant. The energy needed to turn these raw materials into finished products is very cheap and so Bahrain can produce these goods economically.

The Arabian Gulf is a very busy waterway. There are many large oil-tankers and cargo-ships which use the Gulf. The ship-repair yard carries out all kinds of repairs on these large ships. The coast area to the north of Bahrain has been dredged to allow large cargo-vessels to unload at Mina Sulman. This is a container-port with modern facilities and large warehouses which store the many goods that are imported into Bahrain. Smaller *dhows* and other boats can anchor at Mina Manama and Muharraq. (*Mina* means "port" or "harbour".) The fishing-boats also set out from these ports. They usually fish at night and bring back their catch in time for the early morning market.

The Bahrain ship-repair yard

Sand and stone dredged up from the sea-bed is deposited round the shoreline to extend the land area of Bahrain. Before dredging, the sea was so shallow that large ships had to anchor offshore and passengers were carried to land in small boats or on the now rare, famous white donkeys of Bahrain. The harbours and airport which are vital links with the rest of the world are not now Bahrain's only link with other countries. The Causeway—a road built over the sea—connects Bahrain to Saudi Arabia. This means that goods of all kinds can be brought into Bahrain by road from other Middle-Eastern countries and from Europe.

Apart from these heavy industries there are also a number of light manufacturing industries. These include the manufacture of disposable hospital equipment, bedding, soft

73

Dredging sand and stone from the sea-bed. These are used in Bahrain's ambitious land reclamation scheme

drinks, chemicals, furniture, paint and paper products. So, as oil runs out and hopefully more gas is discovered, Bahrain will have new industries to help it maintain its prosperity.

Health and Education

Since the discovery of oil, Bahrain has used its wealth to provide benefits, such as free health care and education, for its citizens.

Life in Bahrain in the last century must have been very different from the modern air-conditioned life we know today. Diseases, such as malaria, carried by mosquitoes; typhoid resulting from insanitary conditions and lack of knowledge about hygiene; and eye diseases perhaps caused by the dusty, windy weather, were commonplace. Resulting infirmity, coupled with the absence of adequate cooling facilities, meant that many people died at a young age—hence the need for girls to marry young, as was customary, and raise a family whilst they were still fit and active.

Modern health care first came to Bahrain in 1900 when first the Victoria Hospital and then the American Mission Hospital were opened. Improvements in health and welfare were not immediate, however. In fact, many of the first missionary doctors themselves died from typhoid or malaria. These diseases have now been wiped out almost completely: malaria by spraying with insecticides the stagnant pools in which mosquitoes lay their eggs; and diseases such as typhoid through innoculation and health education. In the past, many sick people must have suffered and even died through ignorance about health and medicines or because of transport difficulties between hospital and village. (There were few roads and even fewer cars until quite recently.)

This has been remedied through an efficient system of local health centres connected to a large modern hospital called Sulmanyia. At these health centres doctors give advice about child care and minor illnesses, since prevention is better than cure. Modern maternity clinics have also been opened with every modern facility to cater for the ever-growing population. Many of the medical staff still come from overseas. However, the College of Health Sciences and the Medical Faculty of the Arabian Gulf University are training Bahrainis as technicians, nurses and doctors to provide for the future needs of the country. Unhappily, the rigours of the past have left their mark; it is still common to see a young boy leading a blind man—perhaps father, uncle or grandfather—through the narrow dusty streets of Manama.

When Islam came to Bahrain it brought a tradition of education and learning which remains to this day. This was firmly tied to religion—boys would go to the mosque to study the *Quran*, and the *Imam* (priest) would be the teacher.

The first modern school for boys opened in 1919 and the first

Bahraini schoolgirls lining up outside their school

for girls in 1928. These were the very first schools in the Gulf
region. Now there are over one hundred and fifty schools in
Bahrain with more than eighty thousand pupils, both boys and
girls. The school day starts at seven o'clock in the morning and
finishes for the day at noon. Schools start so early because, in
the summer, it gets extremely hot by midday and most people
rest in the hot afternoons. Boys and girls go to different schools
for religious reasons. When there is only one school in a village,
boys go to school in the morning and girls in the afternoon.
Children usually start primary school at five or six years of age.
At eleven or twelve they start secondary school.

Some children go to special secondary schools to learn technical or commercial subjects which are in great demand in this part of the world. The girls usually wear a uniform—a beige or dark brown dress—and have their long dark hair tied up in bright green ribbons. (Green is an especially lucky colour in desert lands because it is the colour of leaves and grass.) The boys do not all wear the same uniform. They may choose western clothes, tracksuits, traditional Arab clothes (*thobes*) or boiler suits, depending on their interests. When they finish secondary school at sixteen, seventeen or eighteen, all schoolchildren take a final examination which tests each of the subjects they have been studying. This is known as the *Towjehia.*

When they finish school, some young people start a job straight away; others go on to higher education. If a student does well in the *Towjehia,* he or she may be able to study further in Bahrain or get sponsorship (similar to a grant from a company or the government) to study in America or Europe—usually the United Kingdom.

Students in Bahrain can attend the Gulf Polytechnic, which offers courses in engineering and business; University College, which offers courses in the arts and education; and the College of Health Sciences which trains nurses and hospital technicians. The Arabian Gulf University offers courses for higher degrees, including medicine. The handicapped are also provided for. There is an institute for the blind where blind people receive training for future careers. And Hope House is a special centre for the physically handicapped. This centre has helped to send

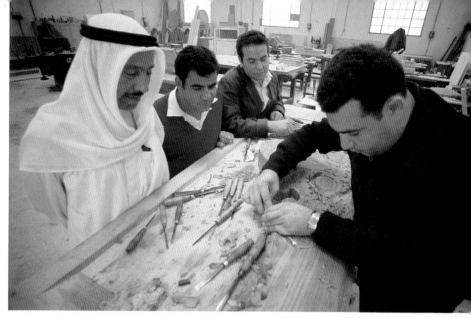

A carpentry lesson in Bahrain Technical School

many handicapped athletes abroad to compete in international events, such as the Handicapped Olympics.

Not only children go to school in Bahrain. Adults go to special centres to learn to read and write. Many older people, especially women, have never been to school. Now they are catching up with their children, and very successfully too. In 1971, sixty per cent of the Bahraini population could neither read nor write. Now this figure has fallen as low as twenty per cent. The government has also started lessons for people from other parts of the world who wish to learn Arabic.

Most Bahraini men seem to know at least one language in addition to their mother-tongue. But the women may not, since they sometimes lead a very sheltered life, mainly within the confines of the home. Arabic, Persian and the Indian languages

79

are frequently heard. Children start learning English at primary school. Nearly everyone on the island, from garage mechanic and car-wash boy upwards, can speak English. This is because English is the international language of business and the one in which Bahrainis and expatriates of all nationalities communicate with each other.

As well as the Arabic media there are two English-language newspapers which are published in Bahrain: the *Gulf Mirror* and the *Gulf Daily News.* In addition, there is an English television channel and two English radio stations, one of which plays the latest pop music.

The Arabic newspapers are called *Akbar Al Kaleej* ("Gulf News") *Al Adhwaa* ("The Light")—both of these are dailies; and *Al Mawakef* ("Views") which is a weekly.

Sports and Recreation

Recreation is very much a family affair in Bahrain. Children playing in an adventure playground are a common sight. Even small villages have parks and playgrounds, full of bright flowers, swings and always a slide. Some of the larger parks in Manama have fun-fair rides, small lakes with ducks to feed and boats to paddle, or perhaps a small zoo—features which are all fairly recent in this part of the world. The parks are usually busiest in the cool of the early evening when families come out to enjoy themselves.

The beaches and the desert are the other main attractions. The two principal beach areas are at Sitra on the east coast and Zallaq on the west. Here there is sunbathing, windsurfing, water ski-ing and sailing. These are very much warm-weather activities even in Bahrain and only the hardiest are to be found in or on the water when the temperature falls below 27 degrees Celsius (80 degrees Fahrenheit).

The government has done a lot to improve the beaches on

Falconry — hunting with birds of prey is a traditional sport in the Arab world, and is still popular in Bahrain today

the north coast nearer Manama. They have landscaped some areas and put up swings. Their efforts have sometimes been hindered by spillage from oil-tankers and refuse from nearby villages which have always regarded the coast as a workplace rather than a place of relaxation. Fishing is now a popular pastime from small boats and from the causeways which join the islands together. Picnics, barbecues and camping are popular with some families; others just sit and watch the sun go down.

All these pursuits may be enjoyed at Ras al Barr, the most southerly tip of Bahrain, forty-five kilometres (twenty-eight miles) south of the hustle and bustle of Manama. Cars usually travel to what is called the "South of the Island" in convoy, in case anyone should get stuck in the wind-blown sand. A police permit is required, to ensure that everyone comes back safely.

For those more interested in animals there is a park south of Zallaq which is the home of many Arabian species, such as the white oryx, and other animals which can survive the harsh climate, including zebra and wildebeest. This is Al-Areen Wildlife Park which was opened in 1976. Al-Areen has strong connections with the Suliman Falcon Centre which is also in the desert. Falconry—hunting with birds of prey—is a traditional sport in the Arab world but it is a sport for the rich, since falcons are very expensive to buy. By contrast, free entrance to the grandstand at Sakhir is affordable by all. Here horse-racing and even camel-racing may be seen in the winter months. Bahrainis are keen horsemen and may be seen riding bareback on their handsome Arab horses along even the busiest of roads.

Darkness falls quickly in Bahrain; perhaps this is one reason

Horse-racing—a sport widely enjoyed in Bahrain

why television is a great favourite. As well as the two national television stations which provide programmes mainly in Arabic and English, there are a large number of video shops which rent out video films in other languages. These have sprung up to cater for the interests of everyone in Bahrain, and have led to a decrease in the number of people attending cinemas.

In Bahrain, modern, international hotels are the place for business entertaining. They have expensive restaurants, floor-shows and performers—or even whole plays—sent out from Europe or the United States. A visit to one of these restaurants is a smart, formal occasion, and the prices are a reminder that Manama is the second most expensive capital in the world after Tokyo, Japan. On a more modest scale are the societies and clubs such as the Bahrain Theatre Club, the Manama Singers, the Garden Club and the Natural History Society. These are open to everyone and they arrange events throughout the year for their members.

There are also a number of important national events which raise money for charity. These include:

The Cherry Tree Trot—a sponsored run/walk for and with the handicapped of Bahrain.

The Red Crescent Bazaar—to raise money for the Red Crescent Society which is the Muslim equivalent of the Red Cross.

The Great Muharraq Raft Race—teams (generally from important companies) compete in a rowing competition, using rafts made out of empty oil barrels—one barrel for each oarsman. This takes place off one of the causeways of Muharraq.

84

Bahrainis are keen sportsmen, and football is the favourite sport. Every village has at least one football pitch where boys play barefoot on the hot, sandy earth. There are also modern, well-equipped sports stadiums where international and local matches are held. These have an enthusiastic following and fans, mostly men, sing, chant and drum. Famous professionals are sometimes brought from other countries to help train Bahrainis and promote sport. Since Bahrain is such a small country, Bahrainis must try doubly hard if they wish to make an impact internationally.

Other sports which are played include cricket, tennis and squash, and golf which has been adapted to desert conditions, having ''browns''—patches of smooth oil-coated sand—rather than the usual ''greens''.

There are many keen runners in Bahrain, and the island has its own marathon. Swimming in the sea and in pools is a good way of keeping cool in summer as is ''ice''-skating—the ice is plastic, coated with a special liquid and does not melt even when the temperature outside reaches 46 degrees Celsius (114 degrees Fahrenheit).

There are certainly plenty of ways of keeping fit and enjoying yourself in Bahrain and there are plans for even more. A large tourist complex is planned for the south-west coast. There will be a theme park and hotel, similar to Disneyland in the United States but with an Arab flavour. This new complex, together with the Bahrain-Saudi Arabian Causeway, should boost tourism to Bahrain and make it a tourist centre for the Gulf.

The Government

Bahrain is governed by the ruler—the Amir Sheikh Isa bin Sulman Al-Khalifa. *Amir* means "Ruler" and *Sheikh* is a title given to male members of the ruling family, rather like "Prince". (The female equivalent is *Sheikha). Bin* means "son of" so the name also gives the name of the Sheikh's father—Sheikh Sulman. Sheikh Isa rules the country with his ministers, many of whom are members of his family. At present they are all men. (Women have little say in government.) The Amir's brother is Prime Minister. His son, Sheikh Hamad, will be the next Amir of Bahrain, as he has been appointed Heir Apparent. He is also Commander in Chief of the Army—the Bahrain Defence Force (BDF). This is very important when there are wars close by.

There are no elections and no parliament in Bahrain. There was a parliament elected by the men (women had no vote) in 1973. But, because of disagreements between the elected members and the government, it was dissolved in 1975.

A painting of the Amir in Hamad Town

Bahrain became independent in 1971. Before that it was a British protectorate. It still has close links with Britain and many British people work on the island. After independence, Bahrain became a member of the United Nations Organization and the International Monetary Fund—a fund which lends money to poor countries.

Although Bahrain has no elected assembly, the Sheikh maintains the tradition of an open *majlis,* as did his father and grandfather. *Majlis* has two meanings: it is the room where a meeting or reception takes place, and it is the meeting or reception itself. At the *Majlis* any Bahraini may speak to the Amir, and ask for help.

87

In 1981, ten years after gaining independence, Bahrain and five other neighbouring states formed the Gulf Co-operation Council (G.C.C.). Other groups of countries have established similar organizations, for example the European Economic Community (E.E.C.). The G.C.C. aims to apply common foreign, economic and defence policies. These are of great importance to the rest of the world because this region supplies a large proportion of world oil. Any country or countries which are rich are looked on enviously by others. For this reason, the Gulf states have decided to join together to remain strong and independent.

The Bahrain—Saudi Arabian Causeway

Of the six countries which signed the Gulf Co-operation Council Agreement on May 25, 1981, Bahrain differed from the rest in one important respect. The other five member-states were all part of the mainland of Arabia, and were connected by a network of roads. Bahrain, being an island, was only linked to the other five by air and sea.

The idea of building a causeway between Bahrain and Saudi Arabia was first discussed as early as 1953. The building of the causeway was actually begun in 1981. A Dutch company won the contract, because the Dutch are so experienced in building dams and bridges in Holland. Work on the causeway was begun from both sides—Bahrain and Saudi Arabia—at the same time. Huge piles were sunk into the sea-bed to serve as the foundations for the enormous bridge. A special cement factory was built on a nearby island to supply the vast amounts of cement required. The causeway is twenty-five kilometres (sixteen miles) long. Saudi Arabia, which is an enormously rich country, has agreed

The causeway which links Bahrain to Saudi Arabia

to pay for this part of the construction. Altogether the total cost of the project will be much higher, including all the link roads, car-parks, etc. which have had to be built.

By the year 2000, approximately thirty thousand vehicles are expected to use the causeway every day, with each one paying a toll for upkeep and maintenance. Even without the causeway, it is estimated that one thousand new cars come onto the roads every month. Because of the impact of so much traffic on such a small island, many car-parks are being built. There are also buses serving Manama and the other main towns. The drive to Saudi Arabia takes about twenty minutes. In addition, it is now possible to drive all the way to the capitals of Europe, most

90

of which are about five thousand kilometres (three thousand miles) from Bahrain.

The building of the causeway is the most important event in Bahrain's history since the discovery of oil. This link with the mainland reverses history, because geologists believe that eight thousand years ago Bahrain was part of the coastline of Arabia.

The Future

The future for Bahrain seems bright. Although the boom years of the 1970s—when the whole Gulf area seemed awash with money because oil prices were high—are over, Bahrain is still a rich country. It has the largest number of Rolls Royces per head of population of any country in the world. Of course, not all Bahrainis drive expensive cars and live in fabulous houses; a few still live in poor shacks and earn very little money. In fact, the oil boom seems to have passed these people by. In between the very rich and the very poor are the great majority of the population who work in factories, offices and shops, and to whom the traditional areas of work—pearling and date-growing—are no more than stories told by their grandfathers.

The biggest task facing the country is to make sure the island maintains its prosperity when the oil-wells have run dry. To meet this situation, Bahrain has encouraged many new industries. But perhaps its best investment is in the children of Bahrain, and in their health and education. In fact, these

92

Bahraini children— Bahrain's hope for the future

young people may also cause the country's biggest problem in the future. Over half the population is under twenty years of age. With the Arabic tradition of large families and more people living longer because of improved health care, this small island could become very overcrowded, quickly using up its most precious resources—water and land.

These are problems which new generations of Bahrainis will have to solve with the help of other Gulf states. Already there are experiments using solar energy (power from the sun), and a great deal of land has been reclaimed from the sea. The future will not be easy but it will be interesting. The hard but tranquil times of the pearl-divers will never return. Since the discovery of oil, Bahrain has become a modern state with both the advantages and the responsibilities which that brings.

93

Index

96